Traverse Theatre Company

One Day All This Will Come to Nothing

by Catherine Grosvenor

Anna	Molly Innes
Paul	Michael Nardone
Adam	Mark Wood
Harriet	Anne Lacey
Martin	Sean Scanlan
Dead Man *Man in Street* *Young Man* *Man in Hostel*	James Cunningham

Director	Philip Howard
Designer	Pip Keppel
Lighting Designer	Kai Fischer
Stage Manager	Lee Davis
Deputy Stage Manager	Gemma Smith
Assistant Stage Manager	Kenna Grant

**First performed at the Traverse Theatre,
Edinburgh, on Friday 18 March 2005**

TRAVERSE THEATRE

Powerhouse of new writing DAILY TELEGRAPH

Artistic Director Philip Howard

The Traverse is Scotland's new writing theatre. Founded in 1963 by a group of maverick artists and enthusiasts, it began as an imaginative attempt to capture the spirit of adventure and experimentation of the Edinburgh Festival all year round. Throughout the decades, the Traverse has evolved and grown in artistic output and ambition. It has refined its mission by strengthening its commitment to producing new plays by Scottish and international playwrights and actively nurturing them throughout their careers. Traverse productions have been seen worldwide and tour regularly throughout the UK and overseas.

The Traverse has produced over 600 new plays in its lifetime and, through a spirit of innovation and risk-taking, has launched the careers of many of the country's best known writers. From, among others, Stanley Eveling in the 1960s, John Byrne in the 1970s, Liz Lochhead in the 1980s, to David Greig and David Harrower in the 1990s, the Traverse is unique in Scotland in its dedication to new writing. It fulfils the crucial role of providing the infrastructure, professional support and expertise to ensure the development of a dynamic theatre culture for Scotland.

The Traverse's activities encompass every aspect of playwriting and production, providing and facilitating play reading panels, script development workshops, rehearsed readings, public playwriting workshops, writers' groups, discussions and special events. The Traverse's work with young people is of supreme importance and takes the form of encouraging playwriting through its flagship education project *Class Act*, as well as the Traverse Young Writers' Group. In 2004, the Traverse took the Class Act project to Russia and also staged *Articulate*, a pilot project with West Dunbartonshire Council for 11 to 14 year olds.

Edinburgh's Traverse Theatre is a mini-festival in itself THE TIMES

From its conception in the 1960s, the Traverse has remained a pivotal venue during the Edinburgh Festival. It receives enormous critical and audience acclaim for its programming, as well as regularly winning awards. In 2001 the Traverse was awarded two Scotsman Fringe Firsts and two Herald Angels for its own productions of *Gagarin Way* and *Wiping My Mother's Arse* and a Herald Archangel for overall artistic excellence. In 2002 the Traverse produced award-winning shows, *Outlying Islands* by David Greig and *Iron* by Rona Munro and in 2003, *The People Next Door* by Henry Adam picked up Fringe First and Herald Angel awards before transfering to the Theatre Royal, Stratford East. Re-cast and with a new director, *The People Next Door* has since toured to Germany and the Balkans. In 2004, the Traverse produced the award-winning *Shimmer* by Linda McLean and a stage adaptation of Raja Shehadeh's diary account of the Israeli occupation of Ramallah, *When The Bulbul Stopped Singing*. This play won the Amnesty International Freedom of Expression Award 2004, appeared in January 2005 as part of the Fadjr International Theatre Festival in Tehran and will go on to tour to New York in Spring 2005.

For further information on the Traverse Theatre's activities and history, an online resource is available at www.virtualtraverse.co.uk.
To find out about ways to support the Traverse, please contact Norman MacLeod, Development Manager on 0131 228 3223.

COMPANY BIOGRAPHIES

James Cunningham (*Missing People*) Trained at the Welsh
College of Music and Drama. For the Traverse: GREEN FIELD,
ABANDONMENT. Other theatre work includes: THE WONDERFUL
WORLD OF DISSOCIA (EIF/Theatre Royal, Plymouth/Tron); PASSING
PLACES (Derby Playhouse/Greenwich Theatre); CLEANSED,
PENETRATOR (Royal Court); YOU'LL HAVE HAD YOUR HOLE (London
Astoria II); MARABOU STORK NIGHTMARES (Citizens/Leicester
Haymarket); TRAINSPOTTING (Citizens). Television work includes:
MURPHY'S LAW (Tiger Aspect); TAGGART (SMG); ROCKFACE (BBC);
BUMPING THE ODDS (Wall to Wall). Film includes: SIXTEEN YEARS
OF ALCOHOL (Tartan Works Ltd); AMERICAN COUSINS (Bard Enter-
tainments Ltd); SNATCH (SKA Films) and WAR REQUIEM (BBC Films).

Kai Fischer (Lighting Designer) Trained in Audio-Visual Media at
the HDM in Stuttgart. Lighting designs for Scottish theatre companies
include: ENDGAME, THE DANCE OF DEATH (Citizens); BEGIN
AGAIN, NEXT TIME AROUND (KtC); THE DANNY CROWE SHOW,
MERLIN (Dundee Rep); EXPLODING CHESTNUTS... (Glasgow
Nürnberg Dance Alliance); WOYZECK, BLOOD AND ICE (Royal
Lyceum, Edinburgh); MARCHING ON (7:84); SWITCHBACK (Sweet-
Scar); STROMA (TAG); MACBETH, A DOLL'S HOUSE, THEBANS,
UNCLE VANYA, MEDEA, GREEKS (Theatre Babel); BEAUTY AND THE
BEAST (Tron/Theatre Babel) and INTO THE DARK (Visible Fictions).
Set and lighting designs include: LOST ONES, SAUCHIEHALL STREET,
STARS BENEATH THE SEA, INVISIBLE MAN, A BRIEF HISTORY OF
TIME, GLIMPSE, LAST STAND (Vanishing Point). Work as Assistant
Lighting Designer includes Scottish Opera's recent productions of DAS
RHEINGOLD and DIE WALKÜRE with Wolfgang Göbbel, LOHENGRIN
(Göteborgs Operan), DIE ZAUBERFLÖTE (Kammeroper Wien), JULIETTA
(Opera North), UN BALLO IN MASCHERA (De Vlaamse Opera,
Gent) and COSI FAN TUTTE with Zerlina Hughes (Scottish Opera).

Catherine Grosvenor (Writer) was born in Edinburgh in 1978.
ONE DAY ALL THIS WILL COME TO NOTHING is her first play.

Philip Howard (Director) Trained under Max Stafford-Clark at the
Royal Court Theatre, London, on the Regional Theatre Young Director
Scheme from 1988-90. Associate Director at the Traverse from 1993-
6, and Artistic Director since 1996. Productions at the Traverse
include 16 world premieres of plays by David Greig, David Harrower,
Catherine Czerkawska, Ronan O'Donnell, Nicola McCartney, Linda
McLean, Sue Glover, Iain Heggie, Iain F MacLeod and the late Iain
Crichton Smith. Fringe First awards for KILL THE OLD TORTURE THEIR

YOUNG, WIPING MY MOTHER'S ARSE and OUTLYING ISLANDS. Other productions at the Traverse include: FAITH HEALER by Brian Friel, THE TRESTLE AT POPE LICK CREEK by Naomi Wallace, CUTTIN' A RUG by John Byrne, WHEN THE BULBUL STOPPED SINGING by Raja Shehadeh/David Greig (also Fadjr International Festival, Tehran) and, as Co-Director, SOLEMN MASS FOR A FULL MOON IN SUMMER by Michel Tremblay (also Barbican Centre, London). Productions elsewhere include: WORDS OF ADVICE FOR YOUNG PEOPLE by Ioanna Anderson (Rough Magic, Dublin); THE SPECULATOR by David Greig in Catalan (Grec Festival, Barcelona); ENTERTAINING MR SLOANE (Royal, Northampton) and SOMETHING ABOUT US (Lyric Hammersmith Studio). Radio: BEING NORWEGIAN by David Greig (BBC Scotland).

Molly Innes (*Anna*) For the Traverse: THE SLAB BOYS TRILOGY, GREEN FIELD, SOLEMN MASS FOR A FULL MOON IN SUMMER, WIDOWS, SHINING SOULS, STONES AND ASHES. Other theatre work includes: GOOD THINGS (Borderline/Byre/Perth Rep); THE MEMORY OF WATER, WIT (Stellar Quines); THE GOOD WOMAN OF SETZUAN, ANTIGONE (TAG); PLASTICINE (Royal Court); BLOODED (Boilerhouse); A LISTENING HEAVEN, JEKYLL AND HYDE, TO KILL A MOCKING BIRD, THE PRIME OF MISS JEAN BRODIE (Royal Lyceum, Edinburgh); TIMELESS (Suspect Culture); DOING BIRD (Cat 'A' Theatre & UK Tour); PLAYBOY OF THE WESTERN WORLD (Communicado); THE STINGING SEA (Citizens); TARTUFFE (Dundee Rep); JOLLY ROBERT/ GLORIA GOODHEART (Theatre Workshop); HAMLET (National Theatre Workshop). Television work includes: TAGGART (STV); REBUS (Clerkenwell Films); PSYCHOS (Channel 4); LIFE SUPPORT, A MUG'S GAME, STRATHBLAIR, THE FERGUSON THEORY, RAB C NESBITT, TAKIN' OVER THE ASYLUM, TREV AND SIMON (BBC); THE BILL (Thames). Film includes: AFTERLIFE (Gabriel Films); RATCATCHER (Holy Cow Films); STELLA DOES TRICKS (Channel 4); KARMIC MOTHERS (Fresh Films).

Anne Lacey (*Harriet*) Trained in Edinburgh, France and Italy. For the Traverse: DARK EARTH, SHETLAND SAGA, BONDAGERS, THE STRAW CHAIR. Other theatre work includes: MARY QUEEN OF SCOTS GOT HER HEAD CHOPPED OFF, THE HOUSE WITH THE GREEN SHUTTERS, JOCK TAMSON'S BAIRNS, THE CONE GATHERERS, TALL TALES (Communicado); THERESE RAQUIN, THE KILLING OF SISTER GEORGE (Citizens); VICTORIA (RSC); THE GUID SISTERS (Tron). Television work includes: MONARCH OF THE GLEN, HOLBY CITY, TINSEL TOWN, HAMISH MACBETH, DEACON BRODIE, KNOWING THE SCORE, RAB C. NESBITT (BBC); DOCTOR

FINLAY (STV). Film includes: HARRY POTTER & THE GOBLET OF FIRE (Warner Bros); MY LIFE SO FAR (Enigma/Miramax); THIS YEAR'S LOVE (Entertainment Film Distributors Ltd); STRICTLY SINATRA (DNA Films).

Michael Nardone (*Paul*) Trained at Queen Margaret College, Edinburgh. For the Traverse: GAGARIN WAY (also at the National Theatre and The Arts Theatre, West End), EUROPE, MARISOL, BUCHANAN, THE COLLECTION, WIDOWS, THE SPECULATOR (EIF/ Traverse), KNIVES IN HENS (also at the Bush). Other theatre work includes: PERIBANEZ (Young Vic); MEDEA (Theatre Babel); VICTORIA (RSC); WILDMAN, SHINDA THE MAGIC APE, THE MARRIAGE OF FIGARO, MERLIN, MIRANDOLINA, MERLIN PT.2 (Royal Lyceum, Edinburgh); BOUNCERS, CAIN AND ABEL (Chester Gateway Theatre); THE SATIRE OF THE FOURTH ESTATE (EIF). Television work includes: ROME (HBO); STEEL RIVER BLUES (Yorkshire); DOCTORS, HOLBY CITY, SILENT WITNESS, CASUALTY, LIFE SUPPORT, LOOKING AFTER JO JO (BBC); TAGGART, INSPECTOR REBUS, TINSEL TOWN, DOCTOR FINLAY (STV). Film includes: THE MATCH (Rafford Films); CONQUEST OF THE SOUTH POLE (Jar Jar Films); SOFT TOP HARD SHOULDER (Gruber Brothers); BEING HUMAN (Enigma Films).

Sean Scanlan (*Martin*) For the Traverse: LOVE LIES BLEEDING (a co-production with the Tron); WIDOWS, NOT WAVING, THE HARD MAN. Other theatre includes: THE ENTERTAINER (Citizens); THE COSMONAUT'S LAST MESSAGE..., PRATT'S FALL , THOMAS MUIR (Tron); THE GLASS MENAGERIE, LOVE FOR LOVE, TIMON OF ATHENS, TROILUS AND CRESSIDA (Bristol Old Vic); THE LIFE OF STUFF (Donmar Warehouse); VICTORIA (RSC); SOFT SHOE SHUFFLE (Lyric Hammersmith). Television work includes: HEARTBEAT (Yorkshire), TAGGART, TAKE THE HIGH ROAD (STV); TWO THOUSAND ACRES OF SKY (Zenith/BBC); SHERLOCK HOLMES, KAVANAGH QC (Carlton); HAMISH MACBETH, RAB C NESBITT, CASUALTY, PUNCH DRUNK (BBC). Film includes: MY LIFE SO FAR (Enigma Films); BLUE BLACK PERMANENT (Margaret Tait); THE BIG MAN (BSB).

Mark Wood (*Adam*) Will graduate from RSAMD in June 2005. Theatre credits include: LOVE, SEX & CIDER (Jacuzzi Theatre). RSAMD theatre credits include: ALADDIN, TARTUFFE, TWELFTH NIGHT, PERICLES, THE NIGHT BEFORE CHRISTMAS, ELECTRA, SUNBURST FINISH and THE SEAGULL. Film includes: IN A MAN'S WORLD, DISTURBED SILENCE, VENDETTA (Clan Films) and HINDSIGHT (Day of the Dog).

SPONSORSHIP

Sponsorship income enables the Traverse to commission
and produce new plays and to offer audiences a diverse and
exciting programme of events throughout the year. We would like
to thank the following companies for their support:

CORPORATE SPONSORS

B B C Scotland

ANNIVERSARY ANGELS

With thanks to
Douglas Hall of IMPact Human Resourcing for management
advice arranged through the Arts & Business skills bank.
Claire Aitken of Royal Bank of Scotland for mentoring support
arranged through the Arts & Business Mentoring Scheme.
Purchase of the Traverse Box Office, computer network and
technical and training equipment has been made possible with
money from The Scottish Arts Council National Lottery Fund

Scottish
Arts Council
LOTTERY FUNDED

The Traverse Theatre's work
would not be possible without the support of

**Sets, props and costumes for
ONE DAY ALL THIS WILL COME TO NOTHING**
created by Traverse Workshops
(funded by the National Lottery)

Scottish
Arts Council
LOTTERY FUNDED

Production photography by Douglas Robertson
Print photography by Laurence Winram

**For their continued generous support
of Traverse productions the Traverse thanks**

Habitat, Marks and Spencer, Princes Street
Camerabase, BHS, Holmes Place

Catherine Grosvenor would like to thank:
Her three wise men – Douglas Maxwell, Troels Christian Jakobsen
and Philip Howard – and everyone at the Traverse
for being so cool.

TRAVERSE THEATRE – THE COMPANY

ONE DAY ALL THIS
WILL COME TO NOTHING

Catherine Grosvenor

For Lewis Burnett,
Folker Stengel and
Christine Stengel-Littmann
with love

Characters

ANNA, *a police officer, thirty*

PAUL, *a bar owner, mid-thirties*

ADAM, *sixteen*

HARRIET, *Mark's mother, late fifties/early sixties*

MARTIN, *Mark's faher, late fifties/early sixties*

Missing People

DEAD GUY

MAN ON STREET

YOUNG MAN

MAN IN HOSTEL

This text went to press before the end of rehearsals and may differ from the play as performed.

Scene One

A waterfront in an industrial part of a city. The body of a
young man lies washed ashore. He has angel wings tattooed
on his back.

PAUL *enters, crosses to the body and kneels next to it. He runs*
a hand over the dead man's head and back. Like a caress. He
stands and leaves.

Lights up. The same. ANNA, *in police uniform, is looking at*
the DEAD GUY.

ANNA. Fantastic. Male, white, twenties. You could be
    anybody.

DEAD GUY. Shh.

ANNA. You don't have a name.

DEAD GUY. Shh.

ANNA. You don't have a home.

DEAD GUY. Shh.

ANNA. And I bet you don't have a National Insurance number.

DEAD GUY. Shh.

ANNA. I need to know.

DEAD GUY. I know. But you're disturbing me.

ANNA. From what?

DEAD GUY. My peace and quiet.

    Pause.

    Actually, I'm getting kind of bored.

    ANNA *does not respond.*

    I said I'm *bored*!

ANNA. Tough.

DEAD GUY. Bored bored bored bored bored bored bored!

ANNA. Yeah, well, you should have thought about that before you jumped.

DEAD GUY. What makes you think I jumped?

ANNA. You all jump. It's always the same. And then some poor innocent jogger trips over you, hysterical phone calls, oh officer it was terrible, terrible, can I get any compensation, we come down, fish you out, try and figure out who you are, no one's ever seen you or missed you and we put you in a box and burn you and that's that.

DEAD GUY. Thanks. No respect for the dead, you lot.

ANNA. What's to respect?

DEAD GUY. Do you ever smile?

ANNA. No.

DEAD GUY. Shame. You could be almost pretty if you smiled.

ANNA. It's ten past eight on Sunday morning. It's freezing cold. I'm sitting next to a dead guy. I don't feel like smiling.

DEAD GUY. Go on.

ANNA. Fuck off.

Beat.

DEAD GUY. Wonder what Mark's doing right now.

ANNA. Shh.

DEAD GUY. How long's it been now?

ANNA. Shh.

DEAD GUY. He could have told you.

ANNA. Shh.

DEAD GUY. I mean, just a phone call. Or even a text. I don't think that's asking too much.

ANNA. Shh.

DEAD GUY. Don't you tell each other everything?

ANNA. Of course we do.

I mean, not everything. Who tells another person everything?

DEAD GUY. Well, exactly. I don't.

ANNA. I don't.

DEAD GUY. I knew we had something in common.

Beat.

Do you think I look like him?

ANNA. Your face is all swollen. You smell of the river. One of your eyes is missing.

DEAD GUY. Just a little bit?

ANNA. No.

DEAD GUY. But I could be him.

ANNA. No.

DEAD GUY. A little bit.

ANNA. No. He's not like you. He's nothing like you.

DEAD GUY. They found his car yesterday, you know.

ANNA. Don't.

DEAD GUY. But it's true. In a motorway service station near a bridge. A bridge I know quite well.

ANNA. I don't believe you.

DEAD GUY. But I'm right. It's all in that report.

ANNA *takes out a folded-up piece of paper and reads it.*

ANNA. That's not our car.

DEAD GUY. Yes it is.

ANNA. It can't be.

DEAD GUY. Things can always be. It's your registration number, isn't it?

ANNA. Yes. But.

DEAD GUY. Well then.

ANNA. What am I going to do?

DEAD GUY. What do you normally do?

ANNA. Take names. Ask questions. When was the last time you saw him, what was he wearing, was he on any medication, had he ever done anything like this before, blah blah blah, they cry, I take notes, the end.

DEAD GUY. So when was the last time you saw him?

ANNA. Tuesday morning.

DEAD GUY. And now it's Sunday.

ANNA. What's your point?

DEAD GUY. Nothing, nothing.

ANNA *shoots the* DEAD GUY *a dirty look.*

What was he wearing?

ANNA. He was in bed. Nothing.

DEAD GUY. Ah-ha! So had you had sex? That morning?
Night before?

ANNA. That's none of your fucking business.

DEAD GUY. That'll be a no. I like it when police officers
don't get any.

ANNA. Fuck you.

DEAD GUY. Anyway. This is distracting us. Was he on any
medication?

ANNA. No.

DEAD GUY. Was he in debt?

ANNA. No more than anyone else.

DEAD GUY. Had anything like this ever happened before?

ANNA. No.

DEAD GUY. So you last saw him on Tuesday morning, after
you may or may not have had sex with him, and there's no
reason you can think of that he might do something like
this.

ANNA. Yeah.

DEAD GUY. And now it's Sunday.

ANNA. Yeah.

DEAD GUY. So what have you been doing all this time?

ANNA. Nothing.

DEAD GUY. Uh-huh.

ANNA. I've been working. I bought food. I watched TV. I
cleaned the bathroom.

DEAD GUY. You know what I mean.

ANNA. I don't need to do anything. I'm just waiting.

DEAD GUY. For what?

ANNA. For him to come home.

DEAD GUY. Don't be so stupid.

ANNA. What do you know? You don't know anything about him. He'll come back. I know he'll come back. This isn't his way. He's not like you.

DEAD GUY. Yeah. Of course. He just went to the corner shop but it took him a week. It's all just one big practical joke. Really, really funny. He's actually at home hiding under the bed. Ha ha ha ha.

Then again, you could be fishing him out of the river tomorrow.

ANNA *kicks the* DEAD GUY.

ANNA. Shut up!

An offended silence.

Sorry.

DEAD GUY. Didn't hurt anyway.

Beat.

I was only trying to help.

ANNA. Thanks.

DEAD GUY. OK. One last question. Did he take anything with him?

ANNA. Nothing. Everything's still there. Clothes, passport, everything.

Beat.

What am I going to do?

DEAD GUY. Did you say Tuesday morning?

ANNA. Yes.

DEAD GUY. What day is it today?

ANNA. Sunday morning.

DEAD GUY. What have you been doing?

ANNA. What am I going to do?

Blackout.

Scene Two

The countryside, a long way from the nearest town. A stretch of open land, just grass and earth. ADAM enters with a spade. He looks like he has been sleeping rough for a few days. He surveys the ground, decides on a spot, and begins to dig a deep hole. He digs for a while before PAUL enters.

PAUL. What are you doing?

    ADAM jumps at the sound of the voice. He whirls round, looks at PAUL, then turns back and keeps digging. More quickly and more panicked than before. PAUL watches ADAM dig.

    What are you doing?

ADAM. Leave me alone.

PAUL. I can't.

    Silence.

ADAM. Please.

PAUL. I can't.

    ADAM stops digging. PAUL watches him.

    What are you doing?

ADAM. Digging.

PAUL. Why?

ADAM. Just digging. Please leave me alone.

    ADAM starts digging again.

PAUL. But I can't leave you. I fear bad things will happen if I leave you.

ADAM. What are you doing here?

PAUL. I was passing.

ADAM. Round here?

PAUL. Well. Maybe not entirely by accident.

ADAM. So why are you here?

PAUL. I'm not sure yet.

ADAM. Who are you? Is this your land?

PAUL. I'm not from round here.

ADAM. Please. I just want to be alone.

PAUL. I'm not leaving.

ADAM. Have you followed me?

PAUL. Why?

ADAM. To stop me.

PAUL. To stop you what? Digging?

ADAM. You know.

PAUL. I don't know anything. I only know what you tell me.

ADAM. Stop it! Tell me why you're here. Have they found me?

PAUL. Who?

ADAM. I don't know. Anyone. My family. They found me. They sent you to find me. You want to take me back.

PAUL. I don't know your family. I don't know anyone.

ADAM. Stop it stop it stop it please leave me alone!

PAUL. No.

ADAM. Why not?

PAUL. Because I can't.

ADAM. There's not meant to be anyone here.

PAUL. There isn't.

ADAM *gestures towards* PAUL.

Who else is there? What else is there? I can't even see a house. There aren't even any birds.

ADAM. Haven't seen anyone in days.

PAUL. It's beautiful, isn't it?

ADAM. Yeah.

PAUL. Tell me why you're here.

ADAM. I can't.

PAUL. Who am I going to tell?

ADAM. That's not the point. I can't tell anyone. No one's meant to be here. That's how it's got to be. No one else can know. You've got to leave. You've got to go.

PAUL. I'm not leaving you.

ADAM starts to dig again. When the hole is deep enough, he climbs in and begins to pull the earth in on top of himself.

I won't let you do this.

ADAM pulls more earth onto himself.

ADAM. I stole the spade. I'm sorry. Will you take it back? A house back that way. Tell them I'm sorry.

PAUL. Take it back yourself.

ADAM. Please.

PAUL. No.

ADAM keeps pulling the earth into the hole. PAUL climbs into the hole with him.

ADAM. No! You can't! Get out! Get out! Get out! This is mine! Leave me alone!

PAUL. What do you want?

ADAM. The soil. Just want to be under the soil. Don't want anyone to know where I am. Don't want to be found. Ever.

PAUL. OK.

PAUL climbs out of the hole, picks up the spade and begins to bury ADAM. He stops when he has filled all the earth back in. He smoothes over the surface with the spade. Silence. He walks away.

ADAM's head bursts back through the earth. He gasps for air. PAUL crosses back to him.

You see? It's never that easy.

Come on.

I'll take you home.

ADAM. Home?

PAUL. With me. Come with me.

I can't leave you in a hole in the ground.

Blackout.

Scene Three

HARRIET *and* MARTIN*'s house. A nice house in the countryside.*

HARRIET *is watching television.* MARTIN *enters.*

MARTIN. What are you watching?

HARRIET. A documentary. A man. An artist who collects his own shit and makes heads out of it. Shit heads.

MARTIN. We went to see his stuff once. Before the shit phase. With Mark. His thirteenth birthday. Remember?

HARRIET. No.

MARTIN. We got lost on the bus. A homeless person grabbed Mark's hotdog out of his hands. My shoes squeaked on the exhibition floor.

HARRIET. I'm going to go to bed after this.

MARTIN. He hated that exhibition.

Silence.

Is there any wine?

HARRIET. There's always wine. Life is unbearable without wine.

MARTIN *pours wine. They watch television.*

Where were you?

MARTIN. Nowhere. Just walking.

HARRIET. I called the police. Can you imagine. Me calling the police. Then I decided I was stupid and hung up. I think they might arrest me for that. Wasting police time. Expect the sirens any second.

MARTIN. I'm sorry.

HARRIET. Of course, you could be having an affair, that's the other thing I thought of, to cheer me up. Maybe someone will send me photos of you cowering in a dog collar with some rubber-clad woman sticking a broom up your arse, and break my heart. Then demand a lot of money.

MARTIN. We could sell the car.

HARRIET. Or you could have just vanished into thin air.

MARTIN. I'm here now.

HARRIET. I can see that.

MARTIN. It's a beautiful evening. A good sky.

HARRIET. The sky, always the sky. You're not going to find him up there.

MARTIN. You have your wine and the television. I have the sky.

HARRIET. I can imagine no existence happier than this.

The doorbell rings. MARTIN *exits and returns with* ANNA *in police uniform, carrying a bunch of flowers.*

MARTIN. Darling. It's the police.

HARRIET. The police. It's alright, officer, I found him.

ANNA. As in me, the police.

HARRIET. Anna.

ANNA. Happy birthday.

HARRIET. They're beautiful. You shouldn't have.

MARTIN. How are you, Anna?

ANNA. Fine. You?

MARTIN. Fine. Fine.

HARRIET. Are you on duty?

ANNA. No. I finished an hour ago. I drove straight up.

MARTIN. You must be tired. Sit down.

HARRIET. There's wine. Maybe you'd like some wine.

ANNA. I'm driving.

MARTIN. Just a little.

MARTIN *pours wine for* ANNA.

HARRIET. We're watching a documentary. About an artist. I don't remember his name. Martin knows.

MARTIN. Alan Rutter.

HARRIET. Martin has the sky to keep him company. I have the television.

Silence.

ANNA. They've found a body. White, male, twenties. No tattoos. There's a lot of people that could be. But I wanted to tell you. We're waiting for the results of the ID. I've told them to call me as soon as they know.

MARTIN. Will it be tonight?

ANNA. They said it would be yesterday.

HARRIET. I'll watch television whilst we wait. You won't mind.

They sit and watch television.

ANNA's *phone rings.*

ANNA. Anna Sheldon . . . Yes . . . Alright. Thanks.

She turns to the others and shakes her head. They sit and watch television. A programme ends.

HARRIET. Well. It's late. Anna. It was good to see you. I'm going to bed.

ANNA. I'm sorry.

HARRIET. Good night.

HARRIET *exits.*

MARTIN. I'd rather have the sky than nothing at all.

ANNA. I should go.

MARTIN. Have you eaten?

ANNA. I'll get something when I go home. I don't want to trouble you.

MARTIN. Please stay. This house is even bleaker without you.

ANNA. I can't.

MARTIN. You have to eat. Stay. I'll make you something. It's no trouble.

ANNA. I'll stay. But please don't offer me any more food.

MARTIN. I'm sorry.

More wine?

ANNA. I'm driving.

MARTIN. Yes, of course you are.

So tell me.

ANNA. What?

MARTIN. Anything. Tell me anything. Everything. About your life.

ANNA. What is there? I buy food. I eat it. I get up every day, I go for a run, I go to work. I come home. I read books about tiling. I sleep.

MARTIN. Tiling?

ANNA. We're tiling the bathroom. Mark is tiling the bathroom. Nothing special, just blue and white. It's going to look really nice. But you know . . . he's just left it lying all over the floor. All these little pieces. You don't see them. Cut my foot yesterday.

MARTIN. Is it bad? Your foot? I can have a look at it for you.

ANNA. It's fine. Stuck a plaster on it. Doesn't hurt. But I have to learn to tile. I bought a book. I'll get it sorted this weekend.

MARTIN. And what else? What else are you doing?

ANNA. I have plants. I look at them. I hope they're going to stay alive.

Beat.

What about you?

MARTIN. Well. The usual. Well. I mean. Work. There's the dog. The garden. Walk round the village. Say hello to people.

Beat.

Was anything bothering him?

ANNA. Hmm?

MARTIN. Did I say something, or Harriet . . . that might have . . . He hadn't called for a while. I just wondered. You would know, wouldn't you? If something was wrong? Something we'd done. Or said.

ANNA. Nothing was wrong.

MARTIN. Because if there was something, something we could do, or change. Anything. We would do it. He just has to tell us. Anything.

ANNA. There's nothing.

MARTIN. There must be something.

ANNA. But I wouldn't know. I don't know.

Don't blame yourself. It's got nothing to do with you. He talks about you all the time. It's really sweet. Mum and Dad this, Mum and Dad that. I get jealous.

MARTIN. Jealous?

ANNA *looks at him.*

Anna. I forgot. I'm sorry.

ANNA. It's fine.

Beat.

They dusted the car. Did I say? For prints.

MARTIN. And?

ANNA. His. Mine.

MARTIN. Anything else?

ANNA. Nothing. No broken windows, no forced locks, no nothing. The doors were locked. His keys, wallet, phone, all gone. There's nothing wrong with it. It's just a normal car in a service station. I mean, they only noticed it after it had been there for three days. It's like he just went to get a sandwich.

MARTIN. Then what?

ANNA *shrugs.*

I'll get some more wine.

ANNA. But I'm driving.

MARTIN. Don't go. Please.

ANNA *holds out her wine glass.*

Blackout.

Scene Four

A smart bar in the middle of a city. It's early evening and it isn't open yet. PAUL *has the keys and shows* ADAM *in.*

ADAM. Cold.

PAUL. You're just nervous.

ADAM. Is it yours?

PAUL. All mine.

ADAM. Nice. Big. Very . . . shiny.

PAUL. You're shaking.

ADAM. Cold.

PAUL. I'll make you a drink. Anything you want.

ADAM. Can I get a hot chocolate?

PAUL. Cream? Flake? Marshmallows?

ADAM. Please.

    PAUL *makes a hot chocolate.*

PAUL. You can take anything you want from here now. It's
    yours.

ADAM. I don't know how to use the machines.

PAUL. I'll show you. It's not difficult.

ADAM. Someone'll find me.

PAUL. No one will find you. You're safe here.

ADAM. Do you promise?

    PAUL *brings* ADAM *his hot chocolate.*

PAUL. Is that what you want?

ADAM. Yes.

PAUL. Then that's what'll happen. I promise. I'll look after
    you.

ADAM. Why?

PAUL. Why what?

ADAM. Why do you want to look after me?

PAUL. It's what I do.

ADAM. How long have you been here?

PAUL. As long as I can remember.

ADAM. Are there lots of people?

PAUL. Where?

ADAM. Here. At night.

PAUL. Yes.

ADAM. What are they like?

PAUL. Young. Rich. White. Blonde.

ADAM. What do they do?

PAUL. Drink. Smoke. Laugh. Leave.

ADAM. Nice.

Beat.

PAUL. I'm going to call you Adam.

ADAM. OK.

PAUL. Tell me a truth about yourself. Adam.

PAUL takes ADAM's jacket off.

ADAM. My name's not Adam.

PAUL takes ADAM's shirt off.

I'm sixteen.

PAUL takes ADAM's shoes off.

My bedroom looks out over the sea.

PAUL takes ADAM's socks off.

I'm scared of the dark.

PAUL takes ADAM's trousers off.

I'm scared of other people.

PAUL takes ADAM's boxer shorts off.

I've never even been in a bar before.

PAUL looks at him.

I don't have anything left.

PAUL exits, taking ADAM's old clothes with him. He returns with a pile of neatly folded black clothes which he presses into ADAM's arms.

PAUL. You can wear these and I swear to you no one will ever look at you again.

ADAM. What about you?

PAUL. I'm different.

ADAM. And the people in the bar?

PAUL. You open bottles of beer for them, you give them wine, you mix their drinks. You take their money. That's all they want you for. You're nothing to them.

ADAM starts to get dressed. He puts on black boxer shorts, a black shirt, black trousers, black socks and shoes and a black apron which he can't tie properly. PAUL helps him.

Beautiful. Perfect.

ADAM. Me.

PAUL. You.

ADAM. Beautiful. Perfect.

Blackout.

Scene Five

The street. A MAN is unpacking the contents of some plastic shopping bags onto the street. The bags are new and the items are still packed. ANNA approaches him.

ANNA. You can't sit here.

MAN. Why not?

ANNA. It's the road.

MAN. It's the law, you mean.

ANNA. The road's more dangerous.

MAN. Nothing comes this way.

ANNA. What's in here?

MAN. The things. Pinks. Little metal thing. Pinks. Wool. Like for a baby.

The MAN shows ANNA some of the things in the plastic bags. A bottle of expensive shampoo. A lipstick. Cotton wool. A pair of tights. A pair of slippers.

ANNA. Are these yours?

MAN. Yes.

ANNA. Where did you buy them?

MAN. What's this?

He looks at the lipstick.

Smells nice.

ANNA. What are you going to do with it?

MAN. Better hide it.

ANNA. What about these?

She holds up the tights, still in their packaging.

MAN. What are they?

ANNA. You tell me.

MAN. Something for tea.

ANNA. No.

MAN. No. When I get home. Tea.

ANNA. And these?

MAN. Tights. What am I going to do with tights?

ANNA. You could hide them.

MAN. Hide them?

ANNA. What's your name? I'm Anna.

The MAN *shakes her hand.*

MAN. I'm Henry.

ANNA. Pleased to meet you. What's your last name, Henry?

MAN. Were you born here?

ANNA. Yes.

MAN. Here?

ANNA. Down the road. You know where the brewery is?

MAN. I know. Why's all this here? What am I meant to do
with it?

ANNA. I don't know. I don't think it's yours.

The MAN *tries on the slippers. They fit.*

MAN. Stinks.

ANNA. Sorry?

MAN. By the brewery.

ANNA. I like the smell. Did you go shopping this morning?

The MAN *unpacks another bag. Groceries – lettuce, bread, tins, bananas. All fresh.*

MAN. These are nice.

He wiggles his feet.

ANNA. Who did you go shopping with?

MAN. She'll never let me keep these.

ANNA. Who?

MAN. Are you the police?

ANNA. Yes.

MAN. That's no good job. Nothing more dangerous than the law.

ANNA. Do you have a wallet?

MAN. Do you need money?

ANNA. Maybe. Do you have a wallet?

MAN. Who are you?! Show me this, show me that. I won't show you anything. Leave me alone.

ANNA. Look. This is my wallet.

The MAN *takes her wallet.*

MAN. Don't have much money.

ANNA. No.

The MAN *takes out his wallet and puts it on the ground. He takes out everything in* ANNA*'s wallet and puts it on the ground.* ANNA *takes the* MAN*'s wallet and opens it.*

You don't have much more money than I do. You don't have any cards. You've got a piece of red string and a stamp and a key. And a library card. I can't read this. What does this say?

MAN. Andrew Phillips.

ANNA. Is that you? Andrew Phillips?

The MAN *shakes his head.*

How are we going to get you home?

MAN. Little cells. People pointing at you. Nasty. I'm not
     going back.

ANNA. Would you rather sit here?

The MAN *wriggles his feet again.*

MAN. Can I keep these?

ANNA. Can I have my wallet back?

Blackout.

Scene Six

The bar. PAUL *is doing paperwork.* ADAM *is mopping the
floor. He keeps banging the mop against the side of the bar,
making a noise. It is clear that he is not used to mopping.
Eventually* PAUL *slams down his books.*

PAUL. Adam!

ADAM. What?

PAUL. What are you doing?

ADAM. Mopping.

PAUL. No, you're not. You're clattering. You're splashing.
     You're muttering. Just mop!

ADAM. I'm sorry.

PAUL. How can you make so much noise?

ADAM. I'm sorry.

PAUL. Stop saying sorry. Just mop.

   ADAM *resumes mopping. He is now especially careful not
   to make a sound and keeps a watchful eye on* PAUL. PAUL
   returns to his books and looks up after a while to see
   ADAM *watching him nervously.*

   What?

ADAM. I don't want to make you angry. I'm sorry. Why are
     you angry?

PAUL. I'm not angry. I just want you to be quiet.

ADAM. OK.

But I don't understand. I don't know what you want. What
am I meant to do?

PAUL. Just mop! Don't think! Don't look at me! Christ, I
should have left you where I fucking found you.

ADAM. No. I want to be here. I'm glad you took me. I'm
going to work really hard. I just never. I never mopped
before. That's not because I'm a bad person. Not because
I'm lazy. I'm not lazy. I'm going to work really hard for
you. I'm a good person. But I never mopped before.

PAUL. None of that matters now. Just do it.

ADAM mops on ineffectively.

Right. Give that here.

*PAUL crosses to ADAM, seizes the mop and demonstrates
how he wants it done.*

Push . . . pull . . . push . . . pull . . . cover all the floor, keep
breathing . . . nice . . . easy . . . quiet.

PAUL throws the mop down at ADAM's feet.

Now finish it.

*ADAM begins to mop. Much better than before. PAUL
returns to his paperwork. ADAM mops the whole floor. He
looks at PAUL when he finishes but PAUL does not look up.
ADAM takes away the dirty water and returns. He stands
near PAUL and waits anxiously.*

Glasses.

ADAM. Gl . . . gl . . .

PAUL. Glasses. Need washing. Behind the bar. Go.

*ADAM crosses to behind the bar, finds a basket of glasses
and begins to wash them.*

ADAM. Is this right? Paul?

PAUL looks up briefly.

PAUL. Just wash.

A pause. ADAM washes.

ADAM. Paul?

What . . .

I mean, why?

I mean, what?

What do you want from me?

PAUL *doesn't respond.*

Why am I here? What are you going to do with me?

PAUL *doesn't respond.*

I mean, why me?

Why do you want me?

Do you really want me?

PAUL *stands and crosses to* ADAM. *He stands next to him and helps him wash glasses.*

PAUL. You need to rinse these better.

ADAM. How do I know what you want from me?

PAUL. Then you need a cloth. Give me your hand. Look. Like this.

ADAM. Who are you?

PAUL *puts his hand over* ADAM's *mouth. Gently.*

PAUL. Stop asking questions. Just do it.

ADAM (*muffled*). But why?

PAUL. Because it's easier this way. I'm not anyone. You're not anyone. I don't want anything from you. You can leave at any time. But if you want to stay, you have to stop asking questions.

ADAM. I want to stay.

PAUL. OK. Keep washing.

ADAM. Will you stay here with me?

PAUL. That's a question.

ADAM. Stay here with me. Please.

PAUL. Better.

They wash glasses together.

ADAM. Who's Michael?

PAUL *freezes.*

PAUL. What?

ADAM. Michael. You keep saying his name in your sleep.
It scared me the first time. I thought there was someone else
in the room. But then I realised. Who is he?

PAUL *does not say anything.*

I'm not jealous. You can tell me about him.

PAUL *suddenly grabs* ADAM *tightly – one hand round his
chest, one clamped over his mouth.*

PAUL. I've never said that name. Not in my sleep, not ever.
You'll never hear it again. Do you understand?

ADAM. Mmmm hmmm.

PAUL *grips him tighter until he struggles, then lets him go.*

PAUL. He's no one.

ADAM. Like me.

PAUL. No. Not like you. Nothing like you.

ADAM. I'm sorry.

PAUL. It's not important. Keep washing.

ADAM. I'm sorry.

PAUL. I said. It's not important. Keep washing.

ADAM. I'm sorry.

PAUL. Adam. Keep washing.

ADAM. Yeah.

Blackout.

Scene Seven

HARRIET *and* MARTIN*'s house.*

ANNA *and* HARRIET *sit watching television.*

HARRIET. You didn't bring flowers.

ANNA. No.

Pause.

Did you want any?

HARRIET. What?

ANNA. Flowers.

HARRIET. No.

Pause.

There's food. I should offer you food. Martin does that, doesn't he.

ANNA. I've eaten.

HARRIET. Have you.

ANNA. Takeaway.

HARRIET. There's wine.

ANNA. There's always wine.

Pause.

Can I sell his bike?

HARRIET. Bike?

ANNA. I trip over it every day in the hall. It's not doing anything. No one ever uses it. It's a good bike. I just. It just stands there. I thought I should sell it. I thought I should check. With you. I don't know. Would you mind? It's a good bike.

HARRIET. Hmmm?

ANNA. Nothing. Is there any wine?

HARRIET. There's always wine.

HARRIET exits.

ANNA puts on the news.

HARRIET returns with a bottle of wine and two glasses.

But not the news. Anna. Put something else on.

ANNA. Just the headlines.

HARRIET takes the remote control and puts something else on.

HARRIET. We don't watch the news. Well, Martin does. He has the old black-and-white set out in the garage. But not in here. I want to enjoy myself here. As much as that's possible.

ANNA. They caught that man, did you see?

HARRIET. Talk to Martin. He'll know. I don't know. I watch soaps. Trash, really. It's all trash. But it makes me happy.

They sit and watch television.

MARTIN *enters.*

MARTIN. Anna.

He kisses her.

How are you?

ANNA. How are you?

MARTIN. You know.

Did you drive up?

ANNA. I got the bus. I sold the car.

MARTIN. Have you eaten?

ANNA. Takeaway.

MARTIN. Not really food.

ANNA. It does the job.

HARRIET. Won't you tell us about the sky.

MARTIN. A good sky. A good sky tonight. Very beautiful. I could have stayed longer. The colours always fade. It's such a shame. Every night the same.

ANNA. They caught that man, did you see?

MARTIN. I saw.

HARRIET. But now I want to watch this. Whatever it is.

ANNA. Martin, I want to sell Mark's bike.

MARTIN. His bike?

ANNA. It's just cluttering up the hall. I keep bashing myself on it.

MARTIN. No.

ANNA. He doesn't use it.

MARTIN. No.

ANNA. I just keep bashing myself on it.

MARTIN. If he comes back –

HARRIET. He's not coming back.

MARTIN. If he comes back and you've sold it.

ANNA. I wanted to ask you.

MARTIN. If he comes back.

ANNA. It was just an idea.

I haven't touched anything else.

I just keep tripping over it.

MARTIN. And if he comes back? He comes back and you've sold his bike? What will he think? What does that say?

ANNA. I'm sorry. It was just an idea.

MARTIN. He loves cycling. He's always loved cycling. We've still got his first bike out there in the garage. Stickers of tigers, remember, Harriet, how much he loved tigers. They're still on the bike.

HARRIET. Martin sits and strokes that bike every night, don't you, dear.

Sell the bike, Anna.

It doesn't matter.

Sell everything.

'If he comes back.'

He'll never learn.

ANNA. I'm sorry. I didn't want to upset you. I won't sell anything. I won't sell anything. Look. I should. Go out for a walk or something.

HARRIET. Look at the sky.

ANNA. I'll be back in a bit.

ANNA *exits.*

MARTIN. What's happened to you? You've become . . . like glass. I'm scared to touch you.

HARRIET. Go and stroke his little bike and remember how perfect everything used to be. I'm watching television.

MARTIN *touches* HARRIET.

Blackout.

Scene Eight

ADAM *is having a bath.* PAUL *sits and watches.*

ADAM. Why are you watching me?

PAUL. Because I like to look at you. And baths are dangerous. You could drown.

ADAM. I'm not going to drown. I'm a grown-up.

PAUL. You can drown in an inch of water. And you're only just a grown-up.

ADAM. How old are you?

PAUL. Thirty-two.

ADAM *laughs.*

ADAM. I've got a sugar daddy.

PAUL. Where did you learn that?

ADAM. I don't know. From telly.

PAUL. You shouldn't say things like that. That's not what you're like.

ADAM. Like what?

PAUL. Like a shit film. A brainless blond model.

ADAM. You don't know me. I could have been raised by a family of brainless models. My daddy is a sugar daddy. He bought implants for my mummy and my sister and now they have matching tits. Like melons. He's getting my sister's nose fixed for her Christmas and then we can find her a sugar daddy too and then we'll all be happy. Sugar-daddy family.

PAUL. Shut up.

ADAM. I can't help it. It's how I was raised. Will you scrub my back, sugar pie?

PAUL *stands to leave.*

PAUL. Don't be stupid.

ADAM. OK, I'm sorry.

My family aren't models. My dad works on the rigs. My sister could do with a nose job though. She's ugly.

PAUL. And you?

ADAM. Look at me.

PAUL. I am.

ADAM. I'm ugly too.

PAUL. Stop fishing for compliments.

ADAM. Do you really like me?

PAUL. What do you think?

ADAM. Come here.

> PAUL *moves over to* ADAM.

Kiss me.

> PAUL *kisses* ADAM.

> ADAM *grabs* PAUL*'s head and pushes him underwater.* PAUL *struggles and frees himself.* PAUL *slaps* ADAM *hard.*

PAUL. You stupid fucking child! What the fuck do you think you're doing? Think it's fucking funny? I tell you you can drown in an inch of water and you try and kill me? Do you want me to die?

ADAM. No. I was just playing. I just wanted to have fun.

PAUL. It's not fun.

> PAUL *pushes* ADAM*'s head under the water. He holds him down for several seconds then lets him go suddenly.* ADAM *coughs and gasps for breath.* PAUL *walks away.*

> *Silence.*

I'm sorry. Shit. I'm sorry. Did I hurt you?

ADAM. No.

You could have killed me.

PAUL. That's what I said. You can drown in an inch of water.

ADAM. You wanted to punish me. I made you angry.

PAUL. You did something really stupid. Do you understand?

ADAM. Yes.

PAUL. You're not stupid. You shouldn't do stupid things.

ADAM. No. I just wanted to have some fun.

PAUL. OK.

Come here. I'll wash your hair.

PAUL *sits down behind* ADAM, *opens a shampoo bottle and starts to wash his hair.*

You're doing much better in the bar.

ADAM. Am I?

PAUL. You are. I'm proud of you.

ADAM. Thank you.

I like this. It's peaceful. I like the smell of the shampoo.

PAUL. I like the feel of your hair.

Blackout.

Scene Nine

ANNA's *garden. An overgrown back green in a tenement.*

ANNA *is sitting in the garden, smoking.* HARRIET *enters.*

HARRIET. Who are you speaking to?

ANNA. No one.

HARRIET. There must be someone.

ANNA. There's no one.

There used to be an old man out here sometimes but I haven't seen him in ages. He must have vanished one night when I wasn't looking.

Beat.

HARRIET. I didn't know you smoked.

ANNA. Do you remember when we found that kid in the skip? The boy. Alan. No, Alistair. The one who went missing. He was missing for nine days. I kept telling his parents, you've got to keep hoping. We'll find him. We'll find him. We found him in a skip with his head missing.

HARRIET. Why are you telling me this?

ANNA. We pulled a guy out of a river. We found a girl in a cage in a wardrobe. I never used to smoke.

HARRIET. This place needs weeding.

ANNA. I like it out here. I feel like I can breathe out here.

HARRIET. It's not even really a garden.

ANNA. Maybe not like yours. But it's different here. They're going to pour concrete over it all anyway. They wrote a letter and told us.

HARRIET. They can't do that.

ANNA. 'Course they can. We're going to get a picnic table and benches. No one here wants to weed a garden.

HARRIET. Sometimes I wish they would find Mark in a skip.

Beat.

ANNA. I was thinking that there should be a man here. A wise old man sitting in the corner, smoking a pipe. He could tell me all the answers. He could tell me everything and I would never have another question.

HARRIET. I don't understand.

ANNA. That's OK.

Beat.

I want him to explain something to me. When something terrible happens – a building blows up, a baby gets shot – people stand and look and they put a hand over their mouth. Why would you do that? You should hold your heart, you should cover your eyes. But mouths, I don't understand. People in New York looking up at the sky, hands over their mouths. Why should I hold my mouth? I don't understand.

HARRIET. I don't know, Anna. Why do you ask things like that?

ANNA. Men in Greece let their beards grow long if their child dies. Martin told me.

HARRIET. And what do the women do?

ANNA. He didn't say. I don't know.

HARRIET. Has he told you about his book? His 'sightings' book. Full of little tables and reports. He goes over it every night. Looking for the secret clue.

ANNA. It's something to do.

HARRIET. And now all this travelling. He won't rest until he finds him.

ANNA. Texas.

HARRIET. Texas.

ANNA. Mark would never go to Texas.

HARRIET. No?

ANNA. He hates the heat. He hates the dust. He hates steak. He hates Americans.

HARRIET. He left himself behind. Maybe he likes steak now.

ANNA. Maybe.

I thought he was in Amsterdam.

HARRIET. Martin? No. He spoke to the boy who thought he'd seen him. Couldn't get a word of sense out of him. He was terribly cross.

ANNA. You're so calm about it.

HARRIET. Are you not?

ANNA. I'm never calm any more. I feel like I. I have to do something. I don't know. Maybe like Martin. Just get out. Go.

HARRIET. Martin's like a dog chasing his own tail.

ANNA. But what else am I going to do? I can't stay here. Look at it.

HARRIET. What's wrong with it?

ANNA. It's a shithole. Sorry. The only good thing about this place is the garden and they're going to pour concrete over that. It's just walls. It's just stone. It's nothing to do with me. It's just a house. It's not me. Mark didn't want it. I don't want it either.

HARRIET. Anna. Don't.

ANNA. There's nothing here. Nothing left. I can't afford the rent any more anyway.

HARRIET. We could pay.

ANNA. No.

I'm sorry. I just mean I need to get out for a while. Clear my head. I can't think any more. I don't know what to do any more. Nothing makes sense here.

HARRIET. If you go.

ANNA. I'll come back. Of course I'll come back. That's not what I meant.

HARRIET. How will I know?

ANNA. I promise. I promise.

HARRIET. Come back to the house when Martin's back, when he's followed up every last lead and spoken to every last inhabitant of the town and come home empty-handed again. He'll need someone to swear at about hoax callers. I just turn the TV up. Martin likes it when you're there. You're alive.

ANNA. You're alive.

HARRIET. No. Not like you. You're the last bit of life we have, Anna.

ANNA. I'll come back.

HARRIET. You hold your mouth to keep your breath in. To keep yourself together. Sometimes I worry that if I open my mouth, I'll start wailing like an animal and never be able to stop.

Blackout.

Scene Ten

A street. A police barrier. ANNA is standing in front of the barrier. She is in uniform. It is night.

The YOUNG MAN approaches the barrier. He is bleeding heavily from a head wound and is drunk. He heads straight past the barrier. ANNA stops him.

ANNA. Sorry. The road's closed.

YOUNG MAN. What?

ANNA. You'll have to find another route. This road's closed.

YOUNG MAN. How do you always do this?

ANNA. There's been a fire. The whole street's been evacuated.

YOUNG MAN. Fire?

ANNA. There's been a fire. You can't go down this street. It's closed.

YOUNG MAN. Get off me!

ANNA. What happened to your head?

The YOUNG MAN *ignores her and tries to get past.*

Where do you want to go?

YOUNG MAN. Always the same, all the fucking same.

ANNA. Where do you want to go?

YOUNG MAN. Why should I tell you?

ANNA. Where do you want to go?

YOUNG MAN. You won't know. You can't help me. I've got
stuff to do like, important stuff, you don't care, you don't
know, you don't know shit.

ANNA. Tell me where you want to go and I'll help you get
there.

YOUNG MAN. How? How will you? You help me?

ANNA. I can tell you which streets are still open.

YOUNG MAN. Fuck, you can smell it.

ANNA. What?

YOUNG MAN. The fire. Burning. Is it bad, like?

ANNA. What?

YOUNG MAN. The fire. Don't want anyone to die, eh? Like
that girl, that little girl . . .

ANNA. I don't have any information on casualties.

YOUNG MAN. See how people do that, burn their own kids,
makes you sick.

ANNA. This is just a small blaze in a shop. We've had to close
the road so the fire engines can get through.

YOUNG MAN. Are you going to help me or not?

ANNA. Where . . .

YOUNG MAN. You're all the fucking same! You don't want to
help me, you couldn't give a fuck about me, not me or
anyone – Don't fucking touch me!

ANNA. Stop trying to get past this barrier. This road's closed
and you're not getting through. There's been a fire and no
one is allowed to go down this road. Not you, not anybody.

YOUNG MAN. Fuck you!

ANNA. If you swear at me again, I'm going to arrest you.

YOUNG MAN. Fuck you!

The YOUNG MAN *charges head first at the barrier and crashes into it.* ANNA *follows him down and takes out her handcuffs. The* YOUNG MAN *lies still.* ANNA *backs off. She has blood on her hand. The* YOUNG MAN *is still not moving.*

ANNA. Shit.

ANNA *kneels down next to the* YOUNG MAN *and checks his breathing and his head. She reaches out an arm and rests it on his shoulder.*

Shit.

The YOUNG MAN *regains consciousness and jerks away from* ANNA. *He scrambles to his feet.*

YOUNG MAN. Get away from me! Get the fuck away from me!

ANNA. You're hurt. I'm trying to help you.

YOUNG MAN. Not you or anybody can help me. You're no one. I'm no one. Fuck you. Fuck you.

The YOUNG MAN *staggers offstage.* ANNA *stays kneeling and wipes her hand on her clothes. She looks down at her clothes. She takes off her hat and coat and places them on the ground. She takes off her radio, her belt, her shirt, her badge, her trousers and her shoes and places them all on the ground. She exits.*

Blackout.

Scene Eleven

HARRIET *and* MARTIN*'s house.*

HARRIET *is sitting in front of the television but there is nothing on. She is holding a shoebox.*

MARTIN *enters. He stops and looks at* HARRIET *when he realises she isn't watching anything.*

MARTIN. I can take it into town tomorrow.

HARRIET. What?

MARTIN. The TV.

HARRIET. It isn't broken. There isn't anything on. It's all young blonde women I've never heard of shouting at me in a language I don't understand. That or houses in the sun.

MARTIN. What will you do?

HARRIET. I have no idea. I might write a letter of complaint.

MARTIN. I meant –

HARRIET. I know what you meant.

MARTIN. Another present?

HARRIET. From Anna.

MARTIN. Was she here?

HARRIET. It came in the post.

MARTIN. So you're free tonight.

HARRIET. What do you want?

MARTIN. I've booked a table.

HARRIET. Speranza?

MARTIN. Speranza. By the window. A view down to the lake. Candles. Pasta with truffles. The finest wine I can buy you.

HARRIET. So now you think you can buy my happiness.

MARTIN. Just the wine.

Do you remember the first time we went?

HARRIET. I'm sure you can tell me.

MARTIN. The twenty-third of September, 1979.

HARRIET. You see.

MARTIN. Your thirty-fifth birthday. It was for seven thirty. We were late. You'd lost an earring. The blue ones. Little blue drops in silver. Only those ones would do.

HARRIET. And what happened?

MARTIN. You couldn't find them. I shouted at you. You have fifty pairs of earrings. You wore other ones. Then you had to change your dress, and the shoes, and your make-up. We were an hour late.

HARRIET. I remember.

And Mark?

MARTIN. Mark. Well.

He stops, uncertain.

I don't remember.

HARRIET. I don't believe you.

MARTIN. He wasn't with us. I'm sure he wasn't with us. Was he? I really don't remember.

HARRIET. You're allowed. That's once in thirty years.

MARTIN. We must have got a babysitter.

HARRIET. These are Mark's things.

MARTIN. What?

HARRIET *touches the box.*

HARRIET. It's not my present. From Anna. She sent them. To both of us. Some of Mark's things.

MARTIN. What kind of things?

HARRIET. I don't know. I can't look.

Pause.

She put everything else in boxes.

MARTIN. I know.

HARRIET. In storage.

MARTIN. I know.

HARRIET. She gave me all the important things. Passport, bank details. Another box. She said she threw away his deodorant and his hair gel.

MARTIN. I know.

HARRIET. So I don't know what this is. The odds and ends. The things that didn't fit anywhere else. Here. You open it.

MARTIN. Later. Let's do it later.

HARRIET. Have you bought me a present?

MARTIN. Of course. I'll give it to you at the restaurant.

HARRIET. If I come.

MARTIN. Please come.

HARRIET. And your book?

MARTIN. I can do it tomorrow.

HARRIET. There's nothing on TV.

MARTIN. Caroline.

HARRIET. What?

MARTIN. The babysitter. Caroline. Tom's daughter. She looked after Mark.

HARRIET. We haven't been back.

MARTIN. I know.

HARRIET. What should I wear?

MARTIN. Whatever you like. As long as you're ready by seven.

HARRIET *nods.*

MARTIN *smiles and exits.*

HARRIET *sits and holds the box.*

Blackout.

Scene Twelve

The lounge of a very cheap hostel. ANNA and a MAN are both hanging around. ANNA is wearing cheap clothes that look second-hand.

MAN. You money?

ANNA. Sorry?

MAN. You money for machine?

ANNA. I don't understand.

MAN. You. Money.

ANNA. You want money? Here.

She gives money to the MAN. He exits. He returns with two plastic cups of coffee.

MAN. For you. Machine.

ANNA. For me?

MAN. For you.

ANNA. Thank you.

MAN. Please.

They drink coffee.

What?

He points into the cup.

ANNA. What is it? I think it's coffee.

MAN. Coffee.

They drink.

You live here?

ANNA. Yes.

MAN. Here very bad. Very many . . . bad thing. You stay here one night, OK. I stay three, I stay four. Is downstair, I like. Why you here?

ANNA. Holiday.

MAN. Holiday? Here?

ANNA. A holiday. Something different.

MAN. Here no good holiday. You go other place.

ANNA. Maybe later. I'll go to another place. Other places.

MAN. You husband here?

ANNA. No.

MAN. You children?

ANNA. No.

MAN. No husband, no children? No nothing?

ANNA. No nothing.

MAN. Maydottirday.

ANNA *nods.*

Maydottirday. Here look, beautiful.

He shows ANNA *a photo.*

ANNA. Your daughter?

MAN. Dottir, yes. Day.

ANNA. She's very beautiful.

MAN. Yes, beautiful. Very beautiful. My dottir.

ANNA. How old is she?

MAN. I go police. I see she.

ANNA. Police? Why?

MAN. My dottirday. See she. See her.

ANNA. At the police?

MAN. Yes, police. I make photo. She day.

ANNA. Day?

MAN. Day.

The man mimes shooting himself.

You know gun?

ANNA. Gun?

MAN. Yes, gun. Gun, she day.

He repeats the gesture, then covers the photo with his hands.

She finish. No dottir. Day.

ANNA. She's dead?

MAN. Yes, day. Dead. I go police, make photo. I show my wife. She . . .

He makes a gesture: 'far away'.

She no think dottir dead. I make photo, show her. She need photo. Need see.

I no see dottir long time. Only photo.

ANNA. Are you going to take her home?

MAN. Hmm?

ANNA. Are you going to take her home? Your daughter? Home?

ANNA mimes picking up a child and carrying it.

MAN. Home? My daughter? No. My country, very far. I no money. Leave dottir here. I go my country. Make photo. Only photo. Police make hole. Hole in ground. For dottir.

ANNA. I'm sorry.

MAN. No sorry. Beautiful daughter. I happy. Happy man.

ANNA. You're lucky.

MAN. Lucky?

ANNA. No. I didn't just say that. I can't tell you you're lucky because you know where your daughter is and you can take a photo of her corpse in a morgue somewhere. You're not lucky. Who the fuck do I think I am?

> ANNA *stands up.*

MAN. You go?

ANNA. Yes. Just outside. Just to walk.

MAN. You want?

> *He offers* ANNA *his coffee.*

ANNA. No. Thank you.

MAN. Thank you.

> Here bad city. No good for woman. Go holiday another place.

ANNA. Tomorrow, another place. I'll be OK. It was nice to meet you. Take care.

MAN. Yes.

> ANNA *exits.*
>
> *Blackout.*

Scene Thirteen

The bar, very late at night after closing. PAUL *and* ADAM *are clearing up.*

PAUL. She was about twelve.

ADAM. Fifteen.

PAUL. Don't try and blag your way out of this one. I saw her. She was a little fucking child and you served her. What were you thinking?

ADAM. Like you never do it. There were those girls last week. I saw you. They were never eighteen. You'll serve people if they're pretty enough.

PAUL. We'll get fucking raided. I'll lose my licence. You don't think.

ADAM. I do think. I think all the time. I'm not old enough to drink here. Remember? You want me to look at them and throw them out and I look at them and they're me and I give them drinks.

PAUL. Be quiet. You're being stupid.

ADAM. I'm not stupid.

PAUL. Well, you fucking act like it.

ADAM *drops a glass on the floor. It smashes.*

You see? Get the brush.

ADAM. I do everything you say.

ADAM *exits. While he is gone, there is a loud, persistent knocking at the door.*

PAUL (*shouts*). Tell them to fuck off!

ADAM *comes back in with* ANNA. ANNA *looks cold, tired and drunk.*

What's this?

ADAM. She says she knows you. I think she's lost. I think she's drunk.

PAUL. I don't know her.

ADAM. I just thought –

PAUL. We're closed.

ADAM. I know. But look at her.

PAUL. I don't know her. What's she doing here?

ADAM. Look at her. Just let her sit for a bit. It's raining outside. Please. Paul.

PAUL. We're closed.

ANNA. Can I have a drink?

PAUL. We're closed.

ANNA. But it's a bar.

PAUL. I know.

ANNA. It's raining outside.

PAUL. I heard.

ANNA. Please. I've come a long way. It's late.

PAUL. That's why we're closed.

ADAM *goes to the bar, pours three drinks and gives one to* ANNA.

ANNA. Thank you.

PAUL. What are you doing?

ADAM *holds out a drink to* PAUL, *who takes it.*

ANNA. Nice place.

PAUL. I don't know you.

ANNA. No.

PAUL. So why –

ANNA. I just said that so he'd let me in.

ADAM. I thought she said –

PAUL. It doesn't matter.

ANNA. I'm looking for someone.

ANNA *puts a photo on the table. Neither* PAUL *nor* ADAM *look at it.*

His name's Mark. He has brown hair, green eyes. Average height. Average weight. No scars, no tattoos.

PAUL. We haven't seen him. Sorry.

ANNA. He might have come in one night. Sat and drank something. Asked you for something.

PAUL. He might have.

ANNA. He's very normal-looking. Normal hair, normal face. Brown hair. Green eyes. Nice teeth. He'll be thirty now.

PAUL. We see a lot of people every night.

ANNA. Maybe he was with someone.

PAUL. We wouldn't remember.

ANNA. Just a really normal-looking guy. Nothing special.

ADAM. If he's not special, why do you want to find him?

ANNA. That's not what I meant. I meant he doesn't look special. I mean, very different. I mean, like you might not notice him. But you might. It's very important. I need him.

ADAM. Why?

ANNA. I don't know how to live without him.

PAUL. Look. I'm sorry for you. But we haven't seen him. And
we're closed.

ANNA. Please.

PAUL. Leave.

I can call the police.

ANNA *laughs.*

ANNA. Only when I find him.

ADAM. Why did you come to us? To this bar?

ANNA. Been to all the others. I'll go somewhere else
tomorrow. Nothing else to do.

ADAM. I shouldn't have let her in.

PAUL. No.

ADAM. I'm sorry.

PAUL. Great.

ANNA *crosses to the bar to get another drink.*

What do you think you're doing?

ADAM. Be careful. There's glass down there. I meant to get
the brush. I forgot.

ADAM *exits.* ANNA *pours drinks.*

PAUL. This is my bar.

ANNA. Just one more.

ADAM *returns with the brush and starts sweeping up the
glass.*

ADAM. I forgot about the glass. That was my fault too. I
dropped a glass. You could have cut yourself.

PAUL. Jesus. Stop fussing.

ADAM. I'm just saying.

PAUL. I know. But I've had enough. I want to go to bed. I
want you to leave.

ANNA. But I like it here. It's peaceful here.

ADAM. You go to bed. I'll stay with her.

PAUL. No.

ADAM. You don't trust me.

PAUL. Why should I?

ADAM. I'm too stupid to do anything. Go to bed.

PAUL. You let her in in the first place.

ADAM. Yeah.

PAUL. You see?

ADAM. You told me not to.

PAUL. And you still did it.

ADAM. I felt like she belonged here.

PAUL. Well, she doesn't. No one else belongs here. Just you and me.

ADAM. And Michael.

ANNA. Who's Michael?

ADAM. No one.

PAUL. What are you doing?

ADAM. I'm just saying. He's no one. Isn't he. A kind of no one who hangs about all the time.

PAUL. I've had enough. You're leaving.

PAUL *grabs* ANNA*'s arms and tries to drag her out of the bar.* ANNA *shakes him off.*

ANNA. Let go!

PAUL. Get out!

PAUL *grabs her again, harder.* ANNA *tries to wrestle free. She slips and falls. She cries out.*

ADAM. Leave her alone!

PAUL. Come on. Get up. Let's go.

ANNA. What are you so scared of?

PAUL. Nothing. I just want you to go.

ANNA. Who's Michael?

ADAM. You're bleeding.

ANNA. There's someone else here.

PAUL. There's no one else.

ADAM. There must still be glass lying about.

ANNA. It's like a secret.

PAUL. You don't know what you're talking about. Either of you.

ADAM. He says his name every night in his sleep. Michael. Michael. Michael. Sometimes he says he's sorry. Michael.

PAUL. Adam! That's enough!

ADAM. I'll get a towel. For the blood. And a plaster.

ADAM *goes to the bar.*

ANNA. You know something. Tell me. Please.

PAUL. There's nothing to tell.

ANNA. Please.

PAUL. None of this has anything to do with you or your story.

ANNA. I don't believe you.

PAUL. Fine. If that's what you want. If you think it will make it all better.

I knew him. His name was Mark. He came to me and said he was sick of his life. He gave me money. I made him a passport and booked a flight for him. He lives in Goa now. He does yoga on the beach at dawn and drinks cocktails as the sun sets. He lives with a beautiful local girl. He wishes he could cease to exist for you as you have ceased to exist for him.

ANNA. No.

PAUL. I killed him. I met him in a dark alley one night and killed him. I cut him into a hundred pieces and dumped each part in a different bin. I killed him for no reason. Just because I could. Because I'm a bad man.

ANNA. Stop it.

PAUL. It's what you wanted. I saw him die. I walked with him to a high bridge and he jumped and the sky was cold and the force of the water broke his neck and the sea carried his body far out and it will never be found.

ANNA. This isn't –

PAUL. And you still want to know why. Because you'd made his life unbearable. Because he felt like he would scream if he had to spend one more night suffocating in your stinking bed. Because he didn't know what else to do. Because someone paid him. Because it just seemed like a good idea at the time.

There are no answers. I'm sorry.

ANNA. There are answers. I just have to keep looking.

PAUL. Then I can't help you any more.

ANNA. And Michael?

ADAM. And Michael?

PAUL. I said. There are no answers. Stop asking questions.

ADAM. But you're sorry. You stroke my hair and you say you're sorry, Michael. You did something to him.

PAUL *shakes his head.*

ANNA. But you knew him.

PAUL. It's late. You have to go.

ANNA. I can't go. I can't go.

PAUL. It's alright. You'll learn. It'll be OK. One day.

ANNA. I'll end up like you? That'll be OK?

PAUL. Yes.

ANNA. No.

PAUL *shrugs.*

What do you have? Nothing. A bar. A little boy to run about and do your bidding. Everything's safe here. What do you know? That's not all there is.

PAUL. What else do you think you're going to get?

ANNA. I don't know. But something.

PAUL *laughs.*

PAUL. You think you're special. You think no one has ever experienced pain or loss or love like yours. You think the world owes you something. You think the world has caused your terrible terrible suffering and now it should make it up to you. You still think everything's going to be alright.

ANNA. That's not true.

PAUL. But you're not. You're just like everyone else. You don't get more or less than anyone else. Don't think that what's happened to you makes you special.

ANNA. You don't know what you're talking about. It's alright for you. You work. You have people you love.

PAUL. Where?

ANNA. I don't know. Here. At home.

PAUL. You see? You know nothing about me. What makes you think there's anyone here I love? Why do you think that would make me happy? Why do you think I need that to live?

ANNA. Mine left me.

PAUL. So maybe he didn't love you.

ANNA. Maybe.

PAUL. Doesn't that make it easier?

ANNA. I know he loved me.

PAUL. But he still left you.

ANNA. Why are you like this?

PAUL. I was born this way. It's in my genes. I can't help it. Sometimes people you love leave you. That's it. Deal with it.

ADAM. He's dead.

ANNA. Who?

ADAM. Michael. Paul. Isn't he. He's like a dead person.

PAUL. No.

ADAM. And you killed him. You hurt him.

PAUL. I didn't kill him.

Silence.

He was my brother. He died when I was four. He drowned in the bath. I was running about and my mum was chasing me with a towel and he slipped and hit his head and drowned.

I've never said that before.

He was my twin. Identical. The same. But better.

That's who he was. So now you know. Now will you go. Leave us in peace.

There is a long silence.

ANNA. I'm sorry.

PAUL. Yeah.

ANNA. Do you still see him?

PAUL. Everywhere.

ANNA. The back of every head –

PAUL. On the bus –

ANNA. Buying a newspaper –

PAUL. The supermarket –

ANNA. Digging up the road –

I remember everything.

PAUL. You should try and forget.

ANNA. I remember how he wrote his As. His smell. The scratch of his stubble on my skin. How he bit his nails. The sound of his footsteps. The colour of his eyes.

PAUL. You should try to forget.

ANNA. Sometimes I can still taste him in my mouth. Feel him under my hands.

PAUL. I remember the taste of ice lollies. My mum used to buy them. He didn't like the orange ones. He made me eat them. He got the cola ones. So I taste the orange ones when I think about him. Chemicals.

ANNA. I still hear him breathe next to me. At night. When it's quiet.

PAUL. They're always there. You learn not to hear them.

ANNA. Does it ever go away?

PAUL. No. You can pretend. But no.

ANNA. And what do I do now?

PAUL. There's nothing to do. Give up. Go home.

ADAM. You always say, be careful, you can drown in an inch of water.

PAUL. I know.

ADAM. I thought you sat and watched me because you liked my body.

PAUL. I do.

ADAM. No. You're just scared. You think I'm going to drown. You think that if you sit and watch me it'll all be alright.

PAUL. It's not like that.

ADAM. I'm not a child.

PAUL. I know.

ADAM. I can take care of myself.

PAUL. I rescued you. You needed me.

ADAM. I thought you wanted me. But you don't. You gave me a name and you never say it. You lie in bed at night and say Michael. I want you to fuck me. Not stroke my hair and pretend I'm your brother.

PAUL. You needed me.

ADAM. But not any more. Go away. I don't want to see you again.

PAUL. Don't be like that. Don't say that.

ADAM. I don't need you. I don't want you. Go away.

PAUL. This isn't –

ADAM. Please.

PAUL. Adam.

ADAM. That isn't even my name.

PAUL. I saved you.

ADAM. But now I'm saved. Now it's just me.

PAUL. I'm sorry.

   PAUL *crosses to* ADAM, *kisses him and exits.*

   Silence.

ANNA. I'm sorry.

ADAM. No.

ANNA. Will he be alright?

ADAM. Out there? What do you think?

ANNA. Out there's no good.

ADAM. Safer in here. Let me see your hand.

ANNA. It's OK.

ADAM. I think there's glass in it.

ADAM takes glass out of ANNA's hand.

ANNA. Who is he?

ADAM. It's not important. Stop asking questions.

ANNA. I can't.

ADAM. It's a lot easier.

ANNA. But I need to know.

ADAM. But if there's nothing *to* know?

ANNA. Got to be something.

ADAM. Why?

ANNA. I don't know.

I don't know anything any more. I don't have anything left.

ADAM. You have everything you need.

ANNA. No.

ADAM. There's air. There's water. There's the ground. There's light. There's you. Everything you need is here.

ANNA. It's nothing.

ADAM. But it's a good nothing.

You look tired.

ANNA. I am tired. I can sleep here. Melt into the floorboards.

ANNA lies down on the floor.

There must be water under us. A long way down.

ADAM sits down next to ANNA and takes her head in his lap.

ADAM. You'll be OK.

ANNA. What's your name?

ADAM. Adam.

ANNA. Your real name.

ADAM. I don't remember any more.

ANNA. Can I kiss you?

ADAM. No.

ANNA takes ADAM's hand and presses it to her mouth.

What are you doing?

ANNA. I don't know. It's like being hungry.

ADAM. Some people don't want to be found.

Beat.

I should clean up.

ANNA does not respond.

Are you OK?

He realises ANNA is falling asleep.

Yeah. You should sleep.

I just have to sweep the floor.

You need a pillow.

He moves her head gently from his lap. He takes off his apron, folds it up and places it under her head.

Is that OK?

I'm just going to sweep.

I can do it in the dark.

It's comforting.

Listen.

ADAM starts to sweep the floor.

It's like a lullaby.

It's like breathing.

You'll be safe here.

ADAM keeps sweeping the floor.

Blackout.

The End.

A Nick Hern Book

One Day All This Will Come to Nothing first published
in Great Britain as a paperback original in 2005
by Nick Hern Books Limited, 14 Larden Road, London W3 7ST
in association with the Traverse Theatre, Edinburgh

Cover image: Laurence Winram

Typeset by Country Setting, Kingsdown, Kent CT14 8ES
Printed and bound in Great Britain by Cox and Wyman Limited,
Reading, Berks

A CIP catalogue record for this book is available from
the British Library

ISBN 1 85459 873 2

———— JUS'

HAY
IN THE
MANGER?

Bible Society
Stonehill Green
Westlea
Swindon SN5 7DG
biblesociety.org.uk

First published 2018 by The British and Foreign Bible Society

ISBN: 978-0-564-04747-5

Design and production by Bible Society Resources Ltd, a wholly owned subsidiary of
The British and Foreign Bible Society.

BSRL/6M/2019
Printed in Great Britain

JUST HAY IN THE MANGER?

The deeper meaning of the nativity

CONTENTS

THE MARMITE FACTOR

Some look forward to it. Others dread it.

A nativity play can trigger conflicting emotions in parents, depending on whether they enjoy shopping for royal robes, whether their child is going to be a herald angel or a speechless shepherd, or whether people think religion and raising children should go together in the first place.

Then again, hasn't the nativity always had the Marmite factor?

Back in the ancient Middle East, where Jesus was born, some people celebrated his birth, while others tried to kill him. In our day, those who love the nativity call it 'the greatest story ever told'. Others argue that this is where the problem lies: it is just a story, a fairytale.

Whatever your own feelings about the nativity, there is one thing on which believers and sceptics agree: the story that began in the little town of Bethlehem has shaped the Western world like no other. This fact alone makes it worthy of our attention.

As children and parents across the land gear themselves up for that big moment in the limelight, this short guide will take you back to the real nativity. We'll discover how our plays compare to what we read in the Bible, how much we can know historically about the world into which Jesus was born, and how this ancient narrative and its message of peace on earth might tie in with our own life stories today.

NOT FOR THE
FAINT-HEARTED

About that time the Emperor Augustus gave orders …
Luke 2.1

Tea-towel headgear, baby Jesus dolls and missed cues – as endearing as nativity plays may be, they are nothing like the original. This was a gritty and subversive story, set in a time when ancient Rome ruled the nations with an iron fist.

Back then, Jewish lands were just a backwater of the Roman Empire. There was no Geneva Convention to protect civilians from invading soldiers; there were no universal human rights, no antibiotics or pension plans. Life tended to be short, not sweet.

Add to that the heavy burden of taxation and the ever-present irritation of Roman religion and lifestyle, and you begin to understand why biblical prophecies of the Messiah had begun to capture the Jewish imagination.

This promised 'Messiah' would be a great leader who would bring peace and justice back to the land. So how much longer would God allow Caesar to put Roman boots on holy ground? When would he send the Messiah to drive out the Jews' enemies and establish his rule on earth?

There was a strange rumour about the Roman emperor at the time, Caesar Augustus (63BC–AD14). It said that he was in fact a son of the god Apollo, born ten months after a serpent had visited his mother in her sleep.

Such a mysterious birth would perfectly suit the purpose of turning a mortal ruler into a mythical figure and securing his power. After all, who would dream of provoking Apollo's anger by showing his son, Augustus, anything but unconditional loyalty?

Jesus, the Jewish boy in the manger, was born during the reign of Augustus, and there were rumours that he hadn't been conceived in the usual way. Could he be the promised Messiah?

Naturally, the Messiah would need to be a formidable figure, with oodles of power, charisma and influence. Jesus, on the other hand, was born in the humblest of circumstances. He was a carpenter's son who grew up in a tiny hamlet in Galilee, a place with no political influence to speak of. The first to hear about his birth were not the famous and powerful, but shepherds and foreign star-gazers.

A strange Messiah indeed. Unlike Augustus the 'son of Apollo', Jesus had not come to conquer.

So who was he?

JUST A STORY?

We know he is telling the truth ...

John 21.24

Before we delve deeper into the meaning of 'the greatest story ever told', we ought to ask, is it more than a story? More than the legends of King Arthur or Robin Hood? Are we talking fact or fiction?

In other words, did the nativity happen? Did the baby in the manger grow up? Was there a man called Jesus of Nazareth, who stirred up the wrath of the empire of Rome for proclaiming the kingdom of God?

Of course, the Bible says so; but Bible writers wanted people to believe in Jesus. So did anyone else mention him? Someone less biased?

2,000 years ago, news largely travelled by word of mouth.

Very few people could read and write. There was no reed and parchment shop in every high street. Moreover, to the Romans, the Jewish lands were not terribly important, and only a few historians bothered to write about what was going on in that remote part of the empire.

Little wonder then that, outside the Bible, we have only a handful of written records about Jesus. Yet – and this is the crucial point – these records do exist.

The Roman historian Tacitus (AD56–120) mentions Pontius Pilate, Rome's representative in Jerusalem, having Jesus crucified.

So does the Jewish historian Josephus (AD37–100), who also refers to Jesus' brother, James, and the fact that the Christian movement carried on after its leader's execution.

Tacitus and Josephus are joined by Roman governor Pliny the Younger (AD61–113) and another historian of the empire, Suetonius (AD69–122), though his reference to Jesus is less clear.

In other words, we have famous Roman and Jewish writers in the first century confirming the existence of Jesus. None of them was a Christian. None of them wrote about Jesus so that their readers would believe in him.

The biblical writers and their non-Christian counterparts agree that Jesus of Nazareth was a real person – someone who gathered followers who came to believe in him as the Son of God, and whose young life was cruelly cut short on a Roman cross.

The Jesus story is rooted in history.

ONCE UPON A TIME

When Jesus was born in the village of Bethlehem in Judea, Herod was king.

Matthew 2.1

How do we know when Jesus was born?

There are four accounts in the Bible, called Gospels, each with a different writer's name: Matthew, Mark, Luke and John. Each Gospel dates back to the first century. Each of them gives us insight into the life of Jesus.

Matthew tells us that Jesus was born during the reign of King Herod the Great. Herod died in 4BC, so Jesus must have been born no later than 4BC.

Luke says that the Roman Emperor Tiberius had been on the throne for 15 years by the time the public began to take note of Jesus' teachings and miraculous deeds. Historical records tell us that Tiberius succeeded the Emperor Augustus around AD11.

AD11, the year of Tiberius' enthronement, plus 15 years of his reign, takes us to AD26. Jesus, according to Luke, was 30 years old in AD26; in other words, he would have been born around 4BC.

So Jesus was not born in AD 0! Nor does the Bible say that his birth date was 25 December, the day we celebrate Christmas. That date may go back to a pagan festival of the unconquered sun.

Ancient civilisations had neither stopwatches nor our modern calendar, but they knew that shortly after the winter solstice the days began to get longer. So they marked 25 December as the point when, once again, the sun god was beginning to beat winter darkness into submission.

The early Christians may have taken over this pagan festival, turning the worship of the sun god into worshipping the Son of God.

O LITTLE TOWN OF BETHLEHEM

While they were [in Bethlehem], she gave birth to her firstborn son. She dressed him in baby clothes and laid him on a bed of hay, because there was no room for them in the inn.

Luke 2.6–7

Jesus grew up in the little town of Nazareth. But Gospel writers Matthew and Luke tell us that he was born in Bethlehem, which was also the birthplace of the iconic King David, who had ruled Israel about 1,000 years earlier. Bethlehem is just south of Jerusalem.

Jesus' family made their home in Nazareth at a later stage. Nazareth is some 70 miles north of Bethlehem.

Nativity plays usually take place in a stable, after Mary and

Joseph have knocked on door after door, and none of the callous, or at best extremely apologetic, innkeepers will let them stay overnight. The Gospel account is much shorter: all it tells us is that Mary gave birth and laid Jesus in a manger, because there was no room in the inn.

Bethlehem, being a small place, probably had no inn or guesthouse in our sense of the word. The 'inn' may have been a normal family home. Houses at the time had an upstairs, where the family slept, and a downstairs for their animals. From the sound of it, the upstairs was full, and Mary and Joseph had to join the animals downstairs.

Nativity scenes tend to place an ox and a donkey in the stable. We can assume that farm animals witnessed Jesus' birth, but the Gospels mention no specific species. Where did the ox and donkey come from?

The prophetic book of Isaiah, written several centuries before Jesus was born, may provide the answer. Using symbolic language, Isaiah says that the ox knows its owner and the donkey knows where its food comes from, but the people of Israel no longer know God because they have drifted away from him.

Ox and donkey next to baby Jesus – humble symbols of the Messiah bringing people back to God?

WE THREE KINGS OF ORIENT ARE

'Where is the child born to be king of the Jews? We saw his star in the east and have come to worship him.'
Matthew 2.2

Stars spend billions of years burning up their fuel. Eventually, as they near the end of their days, they begin to inflate like a balloon, until they either explode or shrink back to a tiny fraction of their former size.

As a star inflates, its glow increases. Seen from earth, a faint star will then appear much brighter, or we may suddenly see a star in the sky where there was none before. Of course, the star has always been there; we just couldn't see it before it began to inflate. Astronomers call it a 'nova', which is Latin for 'new' – a new star.

In the year 5BC, Chinese astronomers observed a bright star – possibly a nova – for 70 days. Might this have been the star of Bethlehem?

Alternatively, the 'star' might have been the planets Jupiter and Saturn, so closely aligned in the sky at the time that they looked like a single bright object.

Nativity plays commonly feature three kings, who follow the star to Bethlehem. Actually, the Bible speaks of 'Magi', or wise men. No doubt, they were priests from Babylonia or Persia, who interpreted the new star as a sign.

The Magi might have been Zoroastrians – followers of an ancient Persian religion – who, interestingly, believed in the coming of a king born from a virgin.

How did nativity plays end up with three kings?

Matthew mentions not three men, but three gifts: gold, frankincense and myrrh. They were given to little Jesus by however many Magi there were.

Each of the gifts gives us a clue about the life and mission of Jesus. Gold represents royalty, frankincense is a sign of priesthood, and myrrh symbolises both healing and burial.

HEROD

Herod secretly called in the wise men and asked them when they had first seen the star. He told them, 'Go to Bethlehem and search carefully for the child. As soon as you find him, let me know. I want to go and worship him too.'

Matthew 2.7–8

Herod the Great's father had been appointed by Julius Caesar to govern the province of Judea. Herod himself was made king of Judea in 37BC by Caesar Augustus.

Herod the Great has gone down in history for two reasons.

Firstly, he was a champion of major building projects such as the expansion of the temple in Jerusalem.

Secondly, he was a tyrant who did not even shy away from having his own family members murdered if he felt threatened.

Herod's cruelty and paranoia chime in with Matthew's Gospel account. When he is told by the Magi about the birth of the Messiah, the king pretends to want to show his reverence for Israel's future ruler. Instead, he orders the killing of all boys up to the age of two, in and around Bethlehem, to ensure that Jesus will not end up competing for his throne.

But Jesus, Matthew tells us, had already been taken to safety.

The events surrounding Jesus' birth are a far cry from our nativity plays. With gritty realism, Matthew exposes Herod's cunning and cruelty.

Meanwhile, Luke in his nativity account exposes another ruthless regime – Rome.

GOOD NEWS FOR WHOM?

That night in the fields near Bethlehem some shepherds were guarding their sheep. All at once an angel came down to them from the Lord, and the brightness of the Lord's glory flashed around them. The shepherds were frightened. But the angel said, 'Don't be afraid! I have good news for you, which will make everyone happy. This very day in King David's home town a Saviour was born for you. He is Christ the Lord. You will know who he is, because you will find him dressed in baby clothes and lying on a bed of hay."

Luke 2.8–12

The nomadic lifestyle of a shepherd in Bible times meant coping with good and bad weather, day and night. Food growing in the wild was scarce. The herd was vulnerable to predators. If you wanted to be a shepherd, you had to be resilient and resourceful.

Shepherds were literally and figuratively on the fringe of society. Their job kept them from observing Jewish purity laws, which made them outcasts in the eyes of pious folk.

These tough outsiders were among the first to visit the Christ child. Not the great and the good in the capital city of Jerusalem, but smelly shepherds in the fields around Bethlehem first heard the angels' message: 'Praise God in heaven! Peace on earth to everyone who pleases God.'

Now what exactly did that mean?

Emperor Augustus, who was on the throne in Rome at the time, had been promoting a similar slogan. 'Pax Romana' stood for peace on earth, Roman style.

The trouble was that Pax Romana (the peace of Rome) meant no more war – but only after the imperial armies had stamped out all opposition. Roman peace meant, 'Don't you dare rise up against us or we will crush you.' Pax Romana was the empire's cynical version of peace on earth.

Instead of an army of Roman soldiers keeping people in check, the nativity story has an army of angels proclaiming peace on earth. Instead of the emperor on his throne in Rome, we get a powerless infant in a manger.

The nativity turned the world, as people knew it, on its head.

'Christ the Lord' is about a different kind of rule: the kingdom of God is not about fear, violence and oppression. It is good news for everyone – peace on a war-torn earth that only God can bring about.

MARY WAS THAT MOTHER MILD

'A virgin will have a baby boy.'
Matthew 1.23

Who was 'that mother mild' in the Christmas carol? Most likely a young teenager.

Back in the first century, a Jewish girl was married off at a very tender age. Agreeing the engagement was up to her father and her future husband. Several months later, she moved in with her spouse.

Mary was engaged to a carpenter named Joseph when the angel Gabriel announced that she would give birth, not to Joseph's but to God's son. A crisis teenage pregnancy if ever there was one.

The moment people discovered she was expecting, Joseph and everyone else would believe that Mary had been with another man. It would mean engagement over, public shame, her very life at risk, with sex outside marriage carrying the death penalty.

Instead of panicking, though, Mary puts her trust in the angel's message and in God's mysterious plan: 'I am the Lord's servant,' she says. Luckily, her fiancé remains loyal against the odds and agrees to help her bring up the child that is not his.

Does all this mean that Mary was just a passive character in a divine plot? Far from it.

For starters, Mary shows enormous resolve and courage. She makes an active choice to go ahead with the pregnancy and to bring up this extraordinary son.

Mary is more than just something to be used. Her willingness to play an active part in God's drama makes all the difference. Little wonder the Gospels give her a more prominent place than Joseph.

At the simplest level, this is a story about a young couple choosing faith and love in difficult circumstances. Yet if that were all, it would hardly have survived the past 2,000 years. The nativity is about God himself touching base with humankind – which finally brings us to the hero of the story.

JESUS

The child Jesus grew. He became strong and wise, and God blessed him.

Luke 2.40

Matthew and Luke devote only a couple of chapters each to Jesus' birth. This gives nativity play writers plenty of room to use their imagination and fill in the blanks. The other two Gospels, Mark and John, do not even mention the nativity, but fast-forward straight to the moment when Jesus begins his life as a travelling teacher and healer.

What matters most to the Gospel writers is the grown-up Jesus: his teachings, his deeds, his crucifixion, and his overcoming of death.

These days, people are less willing to accept miracle stories, so Jesus is perhaps best known for his radical teaching, such as 'Love your enemies and pray for anyone who ill-treats you'. But his ethics cannot be separated from the heart of his message – that God rules; that the world we live in, with all its contradictions, injustices and suffering, will not go on for ever, but the day will come when God puts things right, once and for all.

Jesus was known as a healer and miracle worker; but these were not the magic tricks of a limelight-loving entertainer. Like his words, Jesus' actions pointed towards a greater reality: God mending our relationship with him and healing the earth.

Jesus was a Jew, but he got into conflict with his own religious leaders. The unrest he caused alerted the Roman authorities, who ended up crucifying him. Yet, his death was more than a fateful clash with powerful and ruthless people. Christians came to understand the crucifixion as Jesus taking human pain and wrongdoing upon himself.

At the very beginning, Jesus' first followers seem to have seen in him the promised Messiah sent by God to liberate them from the Romans. There were freedom fighters around at the time who gathered followers, but each of them failed miserably to rid Israel from the foreign yoke.

What would you do if the enemy had defeated the would-be

Messiah you had been following? You would decide that his messianic claims had been false, find yourself another leader, or give up the fight altogether. Remarkably, though, Jesus' followers carried on calling him the Messiah after he had been crucified. Why would they, unless they had become convinced that he had conquered death on Easter morning?

And so, the story that began in a manger in Bethlehem carries on as people today still put their hope in Jesus Christ and his message of God's coming kingdom. In the face of life's difficulties and the certainty of death, they draw strength from his words and presence, eagerly waiting for God to wrap up humankind's tortured history, wipe away every tear and make all things new.

LIKE TO KNOW MORE...?

On the remaining pages of this book, you will find the story of Jesus' birth, taken from the Gospels of Matthew and Luke. If you would like to know more about what Jesus said and did when he grew up, his whole story is told in the four Gospels (Matthew, Mark, Luke and John), which are the first books in the New Testament section of the Bible.

On the Bible Society website, you can find a pocket-sized edition of the Gospels (in the New Revised Standard Version of the Bible): biblesociety.org.uk/pocketgospels

If you would like a copy of the whole Bible, try this pocket-sized edition of the Good News Bible: biblesociety.org.uk/compactgnb

The birth of Jesus in Matthew's Gospel
Matthew 1.18—2.12

This is how Jesus Christ was born. A young woman named Mary was engaged to Joseph from King David's family. But before they were married, she learned that she was going to have a baby by God's Holy Spirit. Joseph was a good man and did not want to embarrass Mary in front of everyone. So he decided to quietly call off the wedding.

While Joseph was thinking about this, an angel from the Lord came to him in a dream. The angel said, 'Joseph, the baby that Mary will have is from the Holy Spirit. Go ahead and marry her. Then after her baby is born, name him Jesus, because he will save his people from their sins.'

So the Lord's promise came true, just as the prophet had said, 'A virgin will have a baby boy, and he will be called Immanuel,' which means 'God is with us.'

After Joseph woke up, he and Mary were soon married, just as the Lord's angel had told him to do. But they did not sleep together before her baby was born. Then Joseph named him Jesus.

The wise men

When Jesus was born in the village of Bethlehem in Judea, Herod was king. During this time some wise men from the east came to Jerusalem and said, 'Where is the child born to be king of the Jews? We saw his star in the east and have come to worship him.'

When King Herod heard about this, he was worried, and so was everyone else in Jerusalem. Herod brought together the chief priests and the teachers of the Law of Moses and asked them, 'Where will the Messiah be born?'

They told him, 'He will be born in Bethlehem, just as the prophet wrote,

"Bethlehem in the land
    of Judea,
you are very important
    among the towns of Judea.
From your town
    will come a leader,
who will be like a shepherd
    for my people Israel."'

Herod secretly called in the wise men and asked them when they had first seen the star. He told them, 'Go to Bethlehem and search carefully for the child. As soon as you find him, let me know. I want to go and worship him too.'

The wise men listened to what the king said and then left. And the star they had seen in the east went on ahead of them until it stopped over the place where the child was. They were thrilled and excited to see the star.

When the men went into the house and saw the child with Mary, his mother, they knelt down and worshipped him. They took out their gifts of gold, frankincense, and myrrh and gave them to him. Later they were warned in a dream not to return to Herod, and they went back home by another road.

The birth of Jesus in Luke's Gospel
Luke 1.26–38 and 2.1–21

God sent the angel Gabriel to the town of Nazareth in Galilee with a message for a virgin named Mary. She was engaged to Joseph from the family of King David. The angel greeted Mary and said, 'You are truly blessed! The Lord is with you.'

Mary was confused by the angel's words and wondered what they meant. Then the angel told Mary, 'Don't be afraid! God is pleased with you, and you will have a son. His name will be Jesus. He will be great and will be called the Son of God Most High. The Lord God will make him king, as his ancestor David was. He will rule the people of Israel for ever, and his kingdom will never end.'

Mary asked the angel, 'How can this happen? I am not married!'

The angel answered, 'The Holy Spirit will come down to you, and God's power will come over you. So your child will be called the holy Son of God. Your relative Elizabeth is also going to have a son, even though she is old. No one thought she could ever have a baby, but in three months she will have a son. Nothing is impossible for God!'

Mary said, 'I am the Lord's servant! Let it happen as you have said.' And the angel left her ...

The birth of Jesus

About that time Emperor Augustus gave orders for the names of all the people to be listed in record books. These first records were made when Quirinius was governor of Syria.

Everyone had to go to their own home town to be listed. So Joseph had to leave Nazareth in Galilee and go to Bethlehem in Judea. Long ago Bethlehem had been King David's home town, and Joseph went there because he was from David's family.

Mary was engaged to Joseph and travelled with him to Bethlehem. She was soon going to have a baby, and while they were there, she gave birth to her firstborn son. She dressed him in baby clothes and laid him on a bed of hay, because there was no room for them in the inn.

The shepherds

That night in the fields near Bethlehem some shepherds were guarding their sheep. All at once an angel came down to them from the Lord, and the brightness of the Lord's glory flashed around them. The shepherds were frightened. But the angel said, 'Don't be afraid! I have good news for you, which will make everyone happy. This very day in King David's home town a Saviour was born for you. He is Christ the Lord. You will know who he is, because you will find him dressed in baby clothes and lying on a bed of hay.'

Suddenly many other angels came down from heaven and joined in praising God. They said:

'Praise God in heaven!
Peace on earth to everyone
    who pleases God.'

After the angels had left and gone back to heaven, the
shepherds said to each other, 'Let's go to Bethlehem and see
what the Lord has told us about.' They hurried off and found
Mary and Joseph, and they saw the baby lying on a bed of hay.

When the shepherds saw Jesus, they told his parents what the
angel had said about him. Everyone listened and was surprised.
But Mary kept thinking about all this and wondering what it
meant.

As the shepherds returned to their sheep, they were praising
God and saying wonderful things about him. Everything they
had seen and heard was just as the angel had said.

Eight days later Jesus' parents did for him what the Law of
Moses commands. And they named him Jesus, just as the angel
had told Mary when he promised she would have a baby.